Purnell
£2.95
UK only

ISBN 0 361 06098 X

Published 1984 by Purnell Books, Paulton, Bristol, BS18 5LQ,
Member of the BPCC Group
Phototypeset by Quadraset Limited
Made and printed in Great Britain by Purnell and Sons
(Book Production) Limited, Paulton, Bristol,
Member of the BPCC Group

Contents

Pink Panther Presents 6
Pink Predators 12
Spots and Robbers 14
Panther's Picnic 20
Rock-a-bye Panther 22
Pink Pursuit 24
A Fruit and Veg Day 26
Police in the Pink 32
Panther's Puzzle Page 34
Inspector Clouseau's Afternoon Off 36
Think Pink 42
A Panther Special 44
Pink Professions 48
Pink Pathways 50
Panther's Fairytale Holiday 52
Pink Playtime 60
Answers 61

The Pink Panther, passing the dazzling window display of the biggest store in town just before Christmas, couldn't help noticing a large sign pasted to the window.

'BENEVOLENT PERSON NEEDED IMMEDIATELY', it read. The Panther was curious.

"Benevolent person? That's me, surely?" he said, purring quietly to himself. "Is there anyone kinder-hearted? Can I pass by without extending the paw of friendship to some needy creature? Not me. And is there, maybe, some chance of a Christmas bonus in this plea for my assistance?"

Quick as a flash he was inside the store and had arranged a meeting with the staff appointments manager on the second floor.

"You won't mind if we keep the door closed and our voices down, will you?" whispered the appointments manager. "Just a moment while I check under the desk."

The Panther looked baffled as the man crawled through the keyhole in the keyhole desk and climbed up on to the chair on the other side.

"Just testing for bugs," the man explained breathlessly. The Panther began to twitch and look around him.

"Not that sort of bug," said the man. "The sort attached to wires which let everyone know what we're saying to each other in this room."

"But we haven't said anyting yet," said the Panther.

"Not yet—but we will, won't we!" said the appointments manager triumphantly. "Now, what makes you think you're a benevolent person, may I ask?"

"I help people," said the Panther, after thinking about it.

"That's good enough for me," said the appointments manager. "You've got the job. Can you start right away?"

"Even sooner," said the Panther. "Er . . . what exactly *is* the job?"

"Christmas, isn't it!" said the appointments manager. "Can't you guess? Red coat, white beard?"

"Entertainments manager, is that it?" beamed the Panther. "Staff concert?"

"Wrong," groaned the appointments manager. "Ever heard of Father Christmas?"

"You don't mean you want me to be your store's Father Christmas, do you?" said the Panther joyfully. "Wonderful!"

"No," said the appointments manager.

"But I thought you said . . ." began the Panther.

"His assistant," said the appointments manager. "He can't sit there talking to all the kiddies and get them their presents too, can he? Turfing them off his knee and dashing off to find them a little parcel—it's just not on! No, what he needs is someone nearby, in the next grotto, so to speak, to hand out the presents as the children leave. See?"

"Yes—now I do," said the Panther. "Do I get to wear a Father Christmas outfit, too?"

"Of course not!" snapped the appointments manager. "Can't have two Father Christmases in one store, can we? The children know it's not the old chap who comes down the chimney on Christmas Eve but they wouldn't expect to see more than one in the store, now would they? No, you'll be all kitted out as a little green gnome."

"Can't I be a little pink gnome?" suggested the Panther. "I'm pink already."

"I can see that," said the appointments manager. "But it really wouldn't do. For one thing nobody ever heard of little pink gnomes and for another, what would you do off-duty? You'd be recognised straight away. No, there's a very nice green jerkin and boots waiting for you in Gents' Outfitting, along with a perky little hat with a feather in it."

While the Panther was off getting dressed for his new role, the appointments manager went along to Father Christmas to tell him about the new assistant. As it was early in the day it was quite quiet in Santa's Grotto.

"Hallo, Jack," said Father Christmas. "Found me a good assistant, have you?"

"There'll be someone along in a minute," said the appointments manager. "But I don't know how good he'll be."

"It's an easy job," said Father Christmas. "All he's got to do is hand out the presents from those boxes over there. Pink for girls and blue for boys. And keep the boxes topped up with gifts so that nobody leaves here empty-handed. Are Packing keeping up with the wrapping up of gifts for the boxes?"

"Yes, I sent down a load of cheap toys yesterday," said the appointments manager. "Oh, here's the new chap now—just in time for your first customer!"

"Hallo, little boy!" said Father Christmas, as a small boy came into the grotto with his mother. "And what would you like for Christmas, then?"

"Stand in here with these boxes," whispered the appointments manager to the Pink Panther, pushing him behind a screen so that the small boy and his mother wouldn't see or hear them. "Have a peep to see if it's a boy or a girl so you'll know what to give them and have the present ready! Then give it to them as they pass by you!"

"OK, sir!" said the Pink Panther. "You can rely on me to give them just what they want!"

The appointments manager hurried away and the Pink Panther looked around him. It was very dark in the grotto, even darker than in Santa's grotto next door, as it didn't have the mass of fairy lights that Santa had around his chair. In the darkness, it was impossible to see the two boxes of cheap gifts cunningly disguised as toadstools . . .

"What I'd really like is a camera," the small boy was saying to Santa. "One that really works and shows the picture straight away."

The Panther's ears pricked up. "Cameras? Where do I get one of those?"

Quick as a flash he was off to the photographic department, where he snatched the first instant camera he could see. "Needed for Santa!" he shouted, waving it at the assistant. "I'd better take a couple more to be on the safe side, it's probably a popular line!"

"What a job this is turning out to be," he said to himself, as he arrived back at his grotto just in time to hand one of the cameras to the surprised child and his even-more-surprised mother. "Still, the man said to give them what they want!"

There was no one else around, so he popped his head round the doorway to have a few words with Father Christmas.

"Get a lot of requests for cameras, do you?" he asked.

"Oh, two or three a day," said Father Christmas. "Computer games, that's what a lot of them want. I never tell them they can have the big things, though. It's not really on, you know."

The Panther didn't see why not, but just then someone came in with some cocoa for the pair of them and he forgot to ask about it.

When he had finished his cocoa, Santa sent him back to the staff canteen with the empty cups.

"Can't have dirty crockery lying about here," he said. "It looks bad. While it's quiet, have a look round the store. I can cope here."

"Good idea," said the Panther. He soon found the canteen from Santa's directions and left the cups there. Then he made his way to computer games. It was very busy in that department but he quickly helped himself to a variety of small games and gave the assistant the appoint-

ments manager's name to explain why he wanted them. The assistant, although surprised at having so much of his stock removed at one fell swoop, was new to the job and was only part-time anyway, during the Christmas rush, so he accepted it without question.

On the way back to the storeroom that was his grotto he picked up a few more suitable gifts—a dolls' house, a couple of bicycles, a wristwatch or two. "Better to be prepared," he said to himself. "Father Christmas might get a rush on this afternoon."

He was right. By lunchtime there was such a crowd outside the grotto that Father Christmas was making them all queue up and come in one at a time.

"Phew!" said the Pink Panther, after a string of children wanting bikes and computers. "What a good thing I got in plenty of stock this morning!"

Down in the store there was a terrible scene going on between the appointments manager and various heads of department.

"What do you mean, I authorised it?" the appointments manager was saying. "I did no such thing!"

"But you did!" they all cried. There was an awful pause.

"What are we going to do about it?" cried the head of the photographic department.

"The scoundrel's giving away all our best items instead of those cheap rubbishy parcels you've got wrapped up and there must be something we can do!"

"Excuse me, sir, but the managing director would like to see you in his office. At once," breathed the worried voice of a secretary in the appointments manager's ear.

He closed his eyes and so missed the sight of the Pink Panther, tiptoeing past. News had filtered through to him that all was not well and he had decided that the best thing to do would be to quietly disappear . . .

"And he'd like to see you, too!" shrieked the secretary, spotting him. All eyes were turned on the Panther. Meekly, he allowed himself to be led towards the store lift behind the dejected man who had engaged him only that very morning.

"Santa's Grotto is closed until further notice!" announced the loudspeaker system in the store. A groan went up in every department.

In the serene atmosphere of the managing director's suite a pin could have been heard to drop, had the floor not been so luxuriously covered in deep pile carpet.

"So you are the two who have revolutionised my trading standards today!" said the big boss, from the vast leather armchair behind the huge desk. Both visitors quavered.

"Wonderful!" boomed the joyful tones of the big boss. "Excellent for business and doubling our takings with every passing minute! Whose idea was it?"

"Er—mine," mumbled the Panther, wishing to take the responsibility. "All my fault, I'm afraid."

"Fault?" cried the managing director. "No fault at all! We can keep this up for the rest of the day!" He paused to study a memo which had been laid on his desk. "No no!" he told his secretary. "Open the grotto again at once! Stock up the gifts! Let them have what they want! Marvellous publicity, you see," he went on. "Gets the customers into the store. They'll buy things then. Let the world know we have the real giving, caring Santa in this store, for the next few days!"

"Well, my friendly gnome," said Father Christmas that night, when the store finally closed. "What do *you* want for Christmas, eh?"

The Panther took off his jolly feathered hat and sat down in a heap on the floor.

"All I want is a new pair of feet and a long, long sleep!" he said wearily.

The Pink Panther is just a lovely big pussycat, of course . . . but he's got lots of fierce cousins in many corners of the world. Big cats are always to be treated with the utmost respect.

Pink Predators

Tiger

Tigers: These can be bigger than any other animal in the cat family. The Siberian tiger can grow to a length of 260cm, with a tail of 112 cm. That's larger than any lion, although anyone near enough to measure it would be better advised not to try!

Lions: Despite being smaller than some tigers, no one disputes the lion's claim to be the King of Beasts. Most lions live in the middle areas of the African continent, although a few may be found in Asia. The lionesses do most of the hunting, fetching their males to have the first feed from any animal they kill.

Lion

Ocelot

Ocelots live in South America, where they hunt in pairs. They climb well, like all cats, but have an added talent; they swim well too and so can go fishing to vary their diet.

Pumas may be called cougars, mountain lions, or even panthers—and in America, where they live, farmers hunt them to save their cattle from attack. Young pumas are spotted, but these spots disappear as the puma grows.

Puma

Leopard

Leopards may be known as panthers and, unlike the puma, this animal stays spotted all its life. The spots make a good camouflage when the leopard is up a tree—and as it eats and sleeps in trees, this is very useful. This is the best climber among the cat family.

Cheetahs can run extremely fast and so live on the fleet-footed antelopes which will outrun other hunters. This big cat differs from the others in that it cannot fully retract its claws.

Cheetah

Wild Cat

European Wild Cat: Even in Britain we have a big cat, although it is rarely seen. Compared to all the other creatures mentioned on these pages the Wild Cat is quite small, but it is much bigger than a domestic cat and more the size of the lynx, which can be found in parts of Europe as well as America. The Wild Cat lives mainly in Scotland, in densely wooded areas well away from humans.

SPOTS AND ROBBERS

The Pink Panther had been to the cinema. After a quiet snooze in the back seat, a whole bag of popcorn and two choc ices, he felt ready to face the world.

"I could lick 'em," he muttered to no one in particular. "I could show 'em what's what! I could bring the underworld to its knees!"

It had been a fast-moving cops-and-robbers film, and the Pink Panther had identified strongly with the tough efficiency of the police force, in the moments when he had been awake.

Dazzled briefly by the sunlight outside the cinema, he strutted proudly into the street. Filled with self-importance, and seeing through the glare of the sun what he took to be the sign on the roof of a taxi, he raised his hand.

"Taxi!" he shouted, stepping off the kerb. The vehicle screeched to a halt beside him, and he was dragged inside. Immediately, the car jolted forward, and he found himself wedged under the front passenger seat, somewhere on the floor of the back of the car.

As if this wasn't bad enough, someone had his foot on him, right in the middle of his chest.

"Er . . . is this really . . . I mean, is this some kind of joke?" queried the Panther, in an effort to keep as calm as possible. "I only wanted to go home—there's no rush."

"Keep your head down, buddy, and don't get smart with us," snarled a voice from the front seat.

The Panther began to feel that he was back in the cinema—only on the screen, with the film.

"What sort of a mistake was that, picking up this guy instead of Charlie?" went on the voice from the front, only this time directed at someone else in the front seat, not the Panther.

"How was I to know?" whimpered the driver. "You know I don't see too good."

He's driving, and he can't see? thought the Panther, beginning to panic.

"But this guy's pink!" shouted the front seat passenger.

"Steady on, you two," said the owner of the foot on the Panther's chest. "It's an ordinary mistake. Charlie was only just getting over Scarlet Fever. He wasn't exactly spotless himself, you know."

"You can shut up, too!" yelled the front seat passenger. "What did you have to drag him into the car for? Look out, Wilf!"

There was a screech of tyres as the car took a corner on two wheels and jumped a small roundabout on the other side. The Panther was, for the first time, glad that he was pinned to the floor by the unfriendly boot, or he would have hit his head on the ceiling.

"Have you got the loot?" asked the driver, when all of them had got their breath back.

"George has, haven't you, George," said the front seat passenger.

"I thought you had it, Harry."

"Charlie's got it!" they all shouted at once, and the Panther gasped as the car swung round yet again and they began to retrace their path.

"It's all your fault for leaving Charlie behind!" yelled Harry, thumping Wilf on the head.

"Er . . . if I may make a suggestion," began the Panther, in the sort of muffled voice that comes with having a knee in your mouth.

"Who asked you?" snarled George, leaning forward to try to pull Harry away from Bert.

"I just thought—" went on the Panther, but got no further. With a wail and a shout, Wilf and Harry fell out of the driver's door on the next bend, followed by George, who had hold of Harry's collar.

The Pink Panther sat up, saw that he was alone in the car and realised the urgent need for someone to drive. Just in time, he grabbed the steering wheel and swung the car away from the fast-approaching stone wall ahead.

"Phew! Sheer skill!" he breathed, mopping his brow and starting to enjoy the driving.

Very soon he was asking himself why he was continuing to drive, and decided to stop. This was easier said than done, as the Panther had never taken driving lessons, and he was having to keep both eyes on the road to avoid the traffic, which was speeding along on his side of the road but in the opposite direction. Just as he realised he was driving on the wrong side, he hit an approaching police car and stopped more suddenly than he would have liked.

He felt his collar being pulled and he was hauled from the car. "Funny thing," he drawled, "but that's how I got in . . ."

"No funny business," said the policeman. "You're coming to the station with me. I should warn you that anything you say will be taken down and may be used in evidence against you."

"Wait a minute!" cried the Panther. "You've got it all wrong! I'm a hero! It's Charlie you should be looking for—he's got the loot!"

"I see, squealing already, are we?" remarked the policeman as he frogmarched the Panther away. "Supergrass, are you? First time I've ever seen pink grass, I must say. Ha, ha!"

The Panther groaned, seeing how hopeless it was going to be to convince anyone of his innocence. Meekly he went into the station.

"I've got the one that did the bank, guv'nor," said the policeman proudly, as he led the Panther into a room where the Inspector sat at his desk.

When the Inspector saw the familiar figure of the Panther approaching he let out an anguished wail and cowered under the desk.

"Is he as bad as all that, guv?" asked the surprised policeman. "If I'd have known, I'd have put handcuffs on him."

"No, no, it's not as simple as that," quavered the Inspector, sitting up again and straightening his tie. "I know this fellow, and while he is certainly not a criminal he is far from a useful help to the officers of law and order in this country."

"You mean he's a plant?" asked the policeman.

"I mean he's a confounded nuisance! Get him out of here," moaned the Inspector.

All the while this was going on, the Panther had been trying to attract the Inspector's attention. He had been visited by an inspiring idea, and he wanted to share it with the Inspector. At last he saw his chance.

"Far be it from me to disagree with you, Inspector," he purred. "But before I go let me give you a vital piece of information. The villains will soon be instantly recognised by the red spots on their faces. In fact, the one with the loot has them already!"

"You mean . . . measles?" gasped the Inspector, leaning forward eagerly.

"No, no, Inspector—you're barking up the wrong disease," said the Panther importantly. He leaned forward too, and lit one of the Inspector's own cigars.

"Scarlet fever! Charlie with the loot has it already and all you have to do is to look out for three other men with spots when another twenty-four hours have gone by!"

Leaving the policemen open-mouthed, he casually strolled out into the sunshine and made his way home, this time unmolested. To be on the safe side, he decided to walk, finding it safer than hailing taxis.

Two days later he judged that by now the villains would have been apprehended and a sizeable reward must have been arranged for him down at the police station. He set out to stroll that way, buying a newspaper from a stall as he went along.

"There may even be a commendation for my bravery announced in this humble rag," he told the newspaper seller, and opened it up to read it.

Surprised at finding no mention of himself by the time he reached the station, the Panther felt a little hurt, and vowed that he would get to the bottom of the matter without delay. He bounded into the police station as he had seen the top policemen do in television dramas, and made his way to the desk. It seemed unusually crowded in the station. There were spotty men all over the place.

"The Inspector? I'm afraid you can't see him today," said the sergeant at the desk. "He's gone home in spots. Come to think of it, I'm not feeling too well myself. And you're looking a bit pink, too. Seems there's an epidemic of Scarlet Fever going around. And most of them have been brought in here accused of bank robbery. I don't see the connection myself, but the Inspector says it was an honest mistake. Sobbing, he was, as they carried him out. Kept muttering something about a Pink Panther—delirium had got him, you see."

The Pink Panther slid quietly out the way he had come, dumping the newspaper in the nearest rubbish bin.

"Who wanted fame, anyway?" he said to himself. "What price rewards? All I ask is the simple life." And he went home to search his chin for spots.

You can have a good picnic anywhere as long as you've picked a safe spot and everyone is prepared to enjoy himself. Wet-day picnics can be just as much fun as sunny ones, if you can find a cosy spot out of the rain—even if it means sitting in the family car or the bus station!

Winter picnics need careful planning—don't sit on the ground and don't stay out too long, either! A hot-water bottle under your coat makes up for not running around while you're eating and if you've got a pair of those sort of gloves which have no ends to the fingers, they're very useful for keeping your hands warm while you eat. Warm drinks and hot soup in flasks make the basis of picnic fare on such occasions.

Here's a list of suitable picnic goodies. No doubt you have your own ideas too!

Tiny sandwiches filled with ham, cheese, sardines, mashed banana, jam, corned beef—practically anything that won't fall out or send the bread soggy. Tiny, because small things are easier to handle.
Sausage rolls. It doesn't matter about crumbs in the open air!

Chocolate crunchies (see the recipe).
Buns—but not sticky ones.
Crisps.
Hard-boiled eggs.
Tiny pork pies.
Slices of cake.
Fresh fruit.

Pink Picnic Tips

Don't take anything to eat that's going to spill all down the front of you, or the picnic will be spoilt while you wonder what sort of trouble you'll be in when you get home. So the best sort of drinks to take are bottles with screw tops and straws, or cartons of juice with straws stuck to the back of them. (Do make sure before you go that yours has a straw, won't you?)

Choose a safe spot. Many a happy picnicker has come to grief through sitting on a nasty nettle or—even worse, but true—a bees' nest. Look first—and make sure you aren't trespassing, or near a busy road.

Leave your dog behind, or he might ruin everything from the picnic spread to the temper of the farmer's sheep in the next field.

Take all your rubbish home with you.

The best sort of picnics are those which take place on glorious sunny days in beautiful locations. The worst sort turn out to be disasters for many reasons—bees and wasps join in too, rain lashes down or all the sandwiches are found floating in spilled orange squash. But somewhere in the middle of all this there is your average picnic which may have its failures but which is a lot of fun, all the same.

RAT TAT
NOW WHO'S THAT? JUST WHEN I'D GOT TO THE EXCITING BIT.
I'M THE FAMILY'S NEXT-DOOR NEIGHBOUR AND I WANT TO KNOW WHAT YOU'RE DOING TO THE CHILD, MAKING HIM CRY LIKE THAT.
ER... NOTHING!
THEN YOU SHOULD BE DOING SOMETHING, - YOU'RE THE BABY-SITTER, AREN'T YOU? HE'S CRYING AGAIN!
WAAARGHHH!
YES, MA'AM!
THERE, THERE, DIDDUMS, - SHUT UP! AARGH!
MY BABY!
WHERE IS THE SCOUNDREL?
NNNN

PINK PURSUIT

The Panther has had some treasure stolen and the Inspector is helping him to get it back. Who will be successful—or will the Villain get away with it?

You need someone to play the Panther, someone else for the Inspector and another person to be the Villain. Each player must have a counter for playing on the board and you'll need a halfpenny to represent the treasure. Dice will be needed too.

The Villain has the first go and he can move off as soon as he has thrown the dice. The Panther and the Inspector, though, must throw a six before they can start; once they have thrown a six, they must throw again to see how many paces they must advance. The first six doesn't count, except to get them started.

When a player lands on a square with instructions for him, he must carry them out if they apply to him, but if he can't for any reason (such as not having the treasure to hide when it tells him to) the instructions must be ignored.

If any player throws a six while in the lead with the treasure, he must go on without the treasure and the next person to throw a six can pick it up.

8
9
VILLAIN HIDES TREASURE IN COPSE AND MOVES ON TO NO12
7
10
6
11
12
14
15
16
VILLAIN COLLECTS TREASURE FROM COTTAGE IF IT'S THERE. REJOINS TRAIL AT NO 12.
17
INSPECTOR OR PANTHER RAIDS COPSE. IS TREASURE THERE?
18
INSPECTOR GETS BAD COLD... MISS A TURN.
13
IF YOU LAND HERE, YOU'LL BE BOUND UP BY VILLAIN'S ACCOMPLICE MISS A GO.
19
20
PANTHER KEEPS FIT.. HAVE ANOTHER GO.
21
VILLAIN GETS TIP, - COLLECTS TREASURE FROM COTTAGE IF IT'S THERE.
28
27
26
PANTHER OR INSPECTOR LEAVE TREASURE IN NEARBY COTTAGE IF THEY HAVE IT.
22
ANYONE HERE LANDS IN DUCKPOND GO BACK TO NO. 15.
25
24
23
41
42
43
44
45
PANTHER CHECKS COPSE FOR TREASURE
INSPECTOR IN COURT. MISS A TURN.
ANYONE LANDING ON THIS SQUARE SNATCHES TREASURE FROM WHEREVER IT IS, AND WINS!

A FRUIT AND VEG DAY

"If I can help somebody, as I pass along," warbled the Pink Panther, as he strolled down town one Saturday morning. "Then my living, has not . . . or is it walk along? Or stroll along? No matter. All the better if it's a job with good pay and prospects, too. Helping one another, that's always been my password to life."

He stopped short as a large sign loomed up, outside a greengrocer's shop.

ASSISTANT REQUIRED. GOOD PAY AND PROSPECTS.

"As I was saying . . ." mused the Panther. He walked in.

There was one man in the shop, serving eight different customers all at the same time. Juggling six oranges into one bag and tossing tomatoes into another, while dealing change to someone else and telling another the price of bananas, he had no chance to notice the languid panther as he lolled in the doorway, watching. But at last the rush was over and he and the Panther were alone in the shop.

"Yes?" said the shopman snappily.

"Come on now!" cried the Pink Panther, leaping into his Best Salesman Approach. "Is this the way to win customers and influence people? A smile, a cheery greeting—"

"No time for that," said the shopman wearily. "Just tell me what you want and I'll weigh it up for you. Speed, that's what you customers want, not smarm."

"Wrong!" bellowed the Panther. "Firstly, I am not a customer."

"Oh yeah?" said the shopman. "Well, if you're reading gas meters, ours is over there."

"I've come about the job," said the Panther. "Assistant. Good pay and prospects."

There was a pause.

"That's different," said the shopman. "Why didn't you say so? Here comes a customer. You can serve this one, and I'll watch and see if you're any good."

"Oh, I'm good," purred the Pink Panther. "Good morning, madam. What is it you need? The finest fruit of our land is spread before you, for only the best is good enough for our customers. And we have peaches from sunny lands afar, strawberries from the other side of the globe—what, just half a pound of onions? Can I not tempt you with—oh, all right then."

"Cut the chat and you'll do fine," said the shopman wearily. "It's such a headache getting help these days. Everyone wants to be a disc jockey."

Side by side, the shopman and the Pink Panther worked hard all morning, weighing and sorting, taking the customers' money and putting it in the till, hauling sacks of potatoes up from the storeroom at the back to replenish the barrels on the counter.

"Is it lunchtime yet?" gasped the Panther, when the scorching sun blazed down from overhead and the lettuces started wilting.

"Lunchtime? So it is," said the shopman. "Grab yourself a carrot and get these orders made up and delivered round the town."

The Panther looked aghast at the huge delivery order which the shopman thrust into his paw. Then he rose to the challenge in true Panther spirit.

Whizz—the fruit and vegetables flew on to the scales and off again, into the bags and boxes, which quick as a flash the Panther loaded on to the truck. Then Zoom! Off drove the Panther, with never a backward glance.

That was a pity, because tied to the back of the truck was a cable which had somehow got itself entangled in the shop's awning—and, as the Panther drove off, the whole of the shop front came crashing down,

knocking the customers flying and sending apples and pears cascading across the street.

Oblivious to the screech of brakes from frantic motorists at the scene of this disturbance, the Panther drove steadily into town on the first of his deliveries.

This was to a restaurant in the better part of town, where notables from the higher walks of life enjoyed good food at exorbitant prices. Pulling up outside, the Panther carefully balanced a box on each paw and backed in through the front door.

Being new to the greengrocery business, he was unaware of the ancient custom of delivering the goods round at the tradesmen's entrance.

Nevertheless, he could not have wished for a better reception.

"Just look at those mangoes, sweetie," cried a large blonde lady to her escort from her table just inside the door. "Wouldn't I just love one of those for dessert!"

"Dirt cheap, too," remarked the ever-eager-to-help Pink Panther, stopping at her table to discuss the produce. He then began a run-down on all the prices of the fruit and vegetables in his boxes, all of which were at least six times lower than the restaurant manager was charging for serving them up.

There began some generally disquieting mutterings among the people at the tables, who seemed somewhat distressed at the profit the restaurant was making out of them. Hearing this, the waiter sent hurriedly into the kitchen for the manager.

"Hey—you!" roared the manager, rushing out from the back in a furious temper.

"Me, sir?" smiled the Pink Panther sweetly.

"Yes, you!" thundered the manager. "What do you think you're doing—trying to ruin me? What kind of a turn do you call that?"

"Turn?" said the Panther. "You mean the cabaret hasn't turned up? Well, I'll do what I can, but it's short notice." He jumped on to one of the tables and began to dance. "I'm not —up to—juggling yet," he gasped, as the boxes of fruit and vegetables began to wobble. "But you can eat what you can catch," he went on, as oranges and potatoes toppled out all over the place. "Oo-er," he said at last, as the manager advanced menacingly towards him. "I was just going—it's a busy day, you know. Sorry I can't stop, but you know how it is. Bye, folks!"

Fortunately the truck started at once, and he was on his way to the next delivery, which was at a large house not far from the centre of town.

The shouts and roars and sound of breaking china should have warned him that some sort of domestic row was already in progress, but, still shaken from the last call, the Pink Panther was not prepared for more upsets. Failing to get an answer to his ring on the bell, he was just about to carry his box of goodies back to the van when the door was flung open and a man rushed past him, closely

followed by a very angry woman. She did not run past the Panther, however, but began to seize everything she could lay her hands on from his box, and throw them at the man, who was now cowering behind the truck.

"Steady on, madam," said the Panther. "Calm yourself. Oh well . . ." He dropped the box on her foot, and leapt into this truck. "Come on, don't be a fool all your life, get in!" he yelled to the man, and together they drove off down the road.

"No, no—I'll have to go back," said the man. "Drop me at the corner here, I can run back."

"Are you crazy or something?" said the Pink Panther in amazement. "That woman's insane. She'll murder you."

"It's just her little way," said the man, jumping out and slamming the door behind him. "But thanks, pal. I'll always buy my vegetables from you in future."

The Panther shrugged and drove on. Last stop of the round was an ice-skating rink, and the Panther had always wanted to go ice-skating . . .

"Shall we try hurling—or is it curling?" said the Panther, after a few glides round the ice. "I've got a load of turnips we could use, in the van." In no time at all he was chucking vegetables around the rink. The trouble was, not everyone had got the idea, and in no time at all there was a heap of bodies tangled together in a wailing heap. "You'll soon get the hang of it," beamed the Panther. "I say, is that the time? Got to go—my lunch-hour's up."

Back at the greengrocers there was a sign up, replacing the one the Panther had seen earlier.

DUE TO COURT ACTION, SUEING, SHOP DISINTEGRATING AND BRAINSTORM PENDING, SHOP IS CLOSED UNTIL FURTHER NOTICE.

The Panther parked the truck and strolled round to the back, where the shopman sat in a shivering heap.

"You!" he muttered in disbelief, as he realised who it was. "Haven't you done enough damage? Come to gloat, have you?"

"What are you talking about?" asked the Panther in genuine surprise. "I've been as quick as I can."

"What about *her*!" roared the shopman, and, looking past him into the shop, the Panther saw the large blonde woman who had thrown his vegetables at the man to whom he had given a lift.

"My mother-in-law," said the shopman. "Seeing you gave her the idea to have a holiday with me. As if I hadn't enough troubles."

"What about my good job with prospects?" asked the Panther.

"Not here, mate!" said the shopman. "Ever thought of becoming a disc jockey? Or any other sort of jockey?"

After reading about the clumsy Clouseau in this book you might be thinking that it's a job you could do a lot better than him! You're probably right . . . but would you be good enough?

You'd need . . . the ability to notice things. Not just the things you were looking at, but other things which you didn't expect to see. Detectives have to be observant; this is how they notice when something isn't quite right.

You'd need to have a good memory, too. Having noticed things which may seem irrelevant at the time, a detective will store all such information away in his or her brain until maybe, at a later date, it will be useful in the search for a criminal.

Detectives need to be able to think quickly and decide what to do in a hurry. A criminal won't wait to be caught and he has an advantage over anyone trying to catch him; he knows he's a wanted man, while other people are trying to find out if he is or he isn't!

Detectives work alongside uniformed police officers in every police station in the country. They often work in everyday clothes and much of their work involves interviewing people, asking questions and following up the replies that they get to these questions. After a burglary, for instance, it is the job of detectives in the CID (Criminal Investigation Division) to try to find out who the burglars were and what they have done with their loot.

Each police station, with its officers, forms part of a regional police force and each force covers just one area of the country. There are about seventy police forces in the British Isles. The police in each area do their best to track down criminals on their own patch, but if they think that

DETECTIVES ARE ENCOURAGED TO STUDY UP THEIR SUBJECTS... THEY NEED TO KNOW WHAT TO LOOK FOR, WHATEVER THE TIME OF DAY OR NIGHT

USING THEIR BRAINS TO TRY TO THINK THEMSELVES INTO THE MIND OF A CRIMINAL...

these criminals have moved out of their area to another one, they can then ask for the help of police in that area to help them. Such a request is never refused, of course—everyone in the police forces throughout the country is dedicated to the fight against crime.

Some detectives, when they have finished their basic training, go on to become expert in one or other of the many departments of their business: fingerprinting, maybe, or art forgeries, stolen cars, or under-water work. Crime intrudes into every aspect of life and many skills are needed in the people who have to fight it. So detectives are encouraged to study up their subjects, so that they become better at their jobs. Nobody can ever tell when a skill might come in useful.

These days, criminals are often caught by the telltale evidence of fibres from clothes, blood stains and many other small things which can be analysed to see if they can help to trace a suspect. Detectives need to know what to look out for, whatever the time of day or night that a crime happens.

Some detectives work in the Fraud Squad, using their brains to try to think themselves into the mind of a criminal. All the time, they are trying to get one step ahead of the criminal in order to catch him.

The job is dangerous—highly dangerous for a lot of the time—and often it means weeks of working in disguise, knowing that at any time that disguise could be spotted, and peril is close at hand. Keeping a cool head is something that a detective has to learn—and every detective at some time needs to be very, very brave.

Detectives try to solve murders . . . prevent burglaries . . . catch bank thieves . . . smash gangs of professional criminals . . . track down forgers . . . trap smugglers . . . and still manage to find the time to be nice and polite to the general public!

PANTHER'S PUZZLE PAGE

As usual, the Panther's up to some tricks! Can you out-smart him?

1 Which way round must these squares fit to un-jumble the Panther?

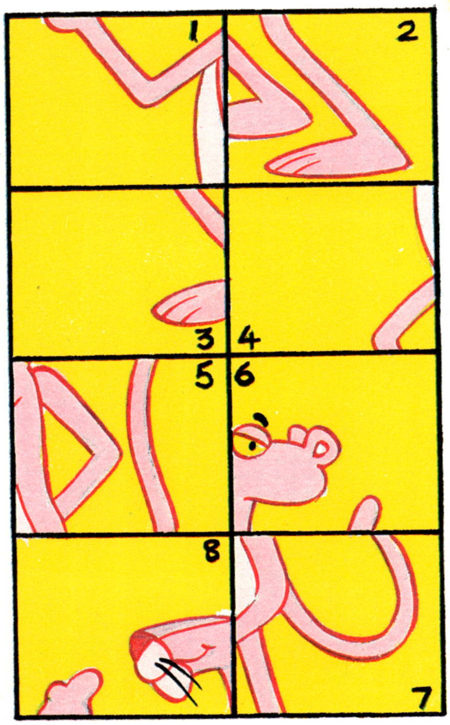

2 Have you got nine pence in one pence pieces? Place them as shown on the table and then see if you can make the arrowhead point in the opposite direction by moving only three coins.

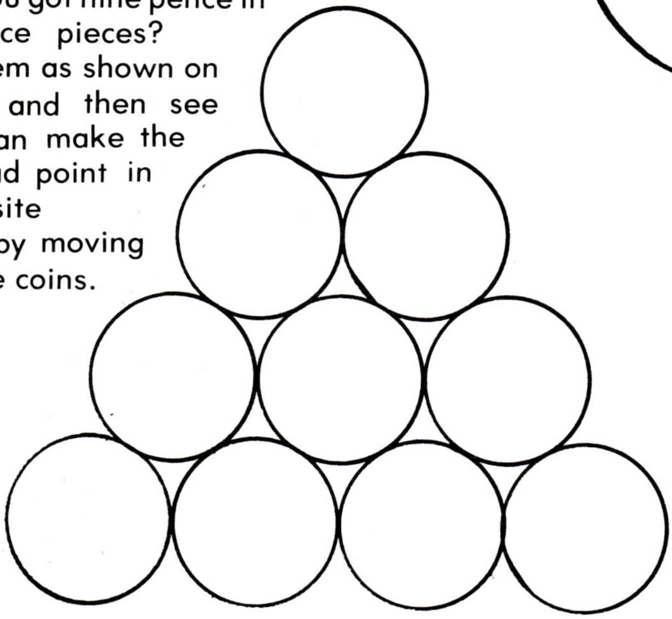

3 Can you draw this face without letting the pencil leave the paper?

4 How musical are you? Here are some muddled-up names of musical instruments—your job is to sort them out.

JONAB
GAUTRI
ANOLDMIN
TEFUL
NOPIA
EBOO
SIRPRAHDOCH
ILIVON

5 Inspector Clouseau has got his men to dress up just like him to fool some villains. Can he fool you too, or will you be able to spot which one is the real Inspector? There's just one vital difference in one of the pictures!

6 Join the dots to find something you might expect to see in wintertime.

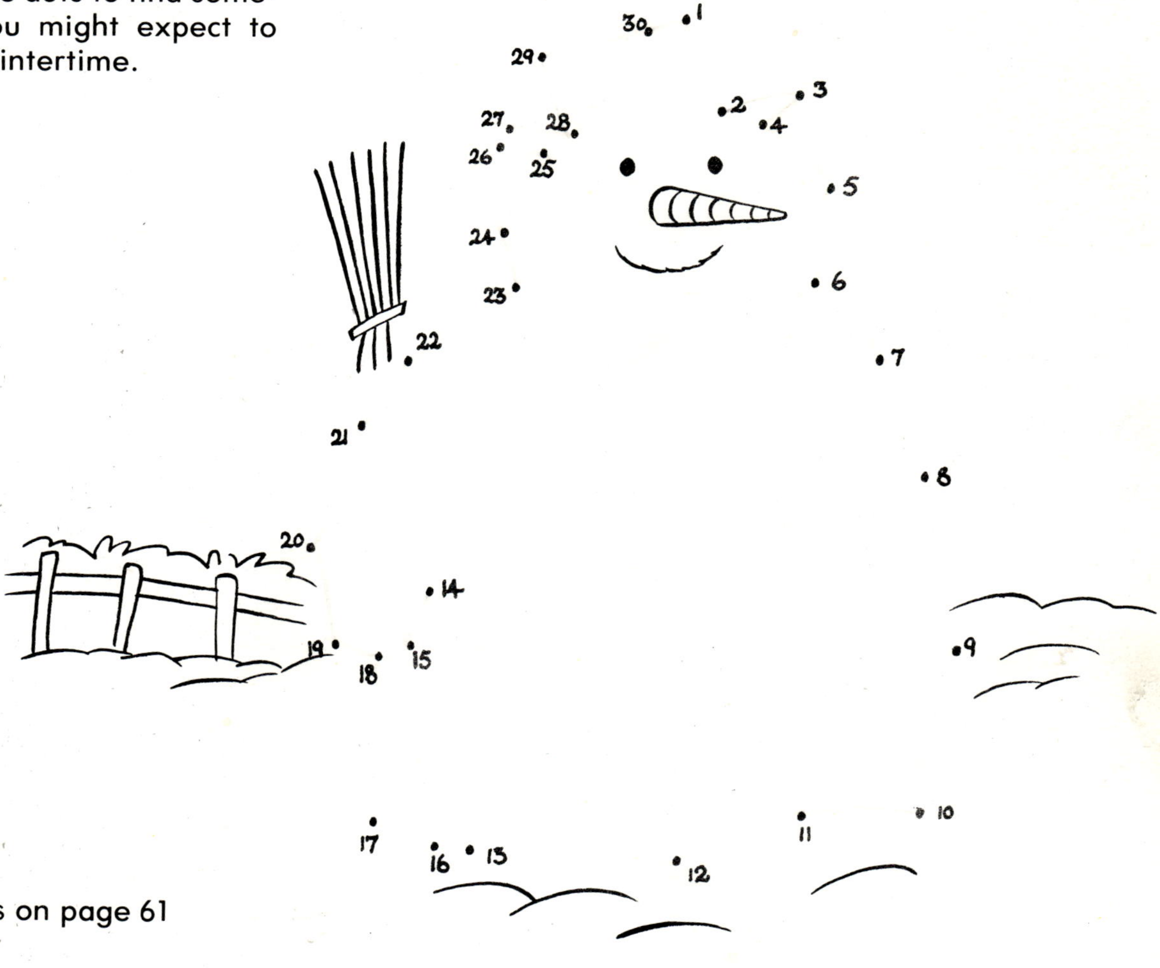

Answers on page 61

INSPECTOR CLOUSEAU'S AFTERNOON OFF

It was a quiet afternoon in the office of Inspector Clouseau. No great dramas had happened. There had been no burglaries, no kidnappings, no buildings set on fire on purpose. It was all very boring for one so highly-strung as the Inspector, and his Chief had found him sobbing at his desk.

"My career is finished!" he wailed. "I have solved all crime! I am done for!"

"Don't be ridiculous!" snapped the Chief, who was not so highly-strung. "This is just a peace wave! Go home and relax, before the criminal underworld starts bothering us again!"

Clouseau wiped away his tears and tried to look on the black side of things once more. Driving home through the city traffic he thought once or twice that a motorist in the queue ahead of him might be planning to break the law by going through a red light or driving on the wrong side of the road, but everyone behaved impeccably.

The Inspector sighed. What was life if there was nothing wrong to put right?

Suddenly, from the bus in front of him, a parcel flew through the air. It came from a top window and landed far from the road, in a lay-by where an open sports car was parked.

"Ha, ha! That's a suspicious package, if ever I saw one," cried the Inspector. With reflexes as sharp as razors, he sliced through the traffic to pull sharply up behind the sports car.

"Time to move on," said the driver of the sports car to his girlfriend, as he stopped kissing her. "Things aren't as quiet round here as they were."

"So they aren't," remarked the girlfriend, looking back at the motorway. "Look at all those piled-up cars! I wonder what happened!"

The reason for the accident watched the sports car drive off, cursing quietly under his breath.

"As I suspected—a getaway car!" he murmured to himself. "This is obviously a well-planned operation. Someone in the bus has thrown the parcel deliberately into the back seat of this sports car, and this man kissing his girlfriend is obviously an accomplice! But ha ha! They have reckoned without me, Inspector Clouseau!"

Revving his engine, the Inspector set off on the trail of the sports car. Because all the traffic behind him was still involved in the giant pile-up, there were no other vehicles on the road and before long he caught up with the courting couple who, without knowing it, were carrying the mysterious parcel in the back seat of their open car.

"It was time we were moving on anyway, dear," said the girlfriend. "You mustn't be late for your performance at the town hall. It would disappoint the children so."

She turned to smile at him and out of the corner of her eye caught sight of a mad motorist driving dangerously near to their back wheel. In his hand was a long fishing rod which he was waving at them.

"Help! Look out!" she cried, as the Inspector veered towards, and then away from, their motor. The fishing rod latched on to the back seat, ripping a gash in the upholstery before swinging free over the driver's head. He ducked, and there was a terrible crunch as the two cars collided.

"He's a maniac!" gasped the sports driver, taking the first available side road to try to escape. Unprepared for this, Clouseau missed the turning and had to plough across an old lady's front garden to get on to the same road. In the few seconds lead this gave him, the sports car driver was able to stop at a nearby telephone box. The girlfriend jumped out.

"Ring the police at once, my dear, and summon their assistance! I will see you later at the town hall!" he cried, driving off again as the Inspector thundered up the road behind him.

"The things we do in the pursuit of crime!" muttered the Inspector as he gave chase. "This is obviously a desperate criminal!" And he revved up his engine even more.

Having rung the police and told them everything about their terrifying ordeal, the girlfriend ran back down the road to the old lady's cottage, where she found the old dear hopping up and down with rage at the mess the Inspector had made of her flowerbeds.

"We will go after him!" roared the old lady, and together they mounted the old lady's motorbike and set off towards the town centre.

It was mid-afternoon by the time the sports car pulled up outside the town hall, and the driver knew that he was somewhat late. Dashing inside he failed to notice the Inspector's car behind him. Thinking himself safe inside the town hall, he rushed upstairs without bothering to close any doors behind him . . .

"Just in time!" beamed a stout vicar, meeting him at the top of the stairs. "This way, if you please . . . I trust you will not take long to prepare yourself."

"Not at all," replied the sports car driver. He had snatched up an armful of equipment from the back seat of the car and now waved it at the vicar. "Everything I need is here."

"Ah ha!" said the Inspector to himself in the darkness of a quiet alcove halfway down the staircase. "That is the parcel in his arms, along with all the other things! This is obviously a fake vicar! I shall lose no time in shutting him in the nearest cupboard before I tackle the other criminal!"

It was a great surprise to the vicar, a few minutes later, to find himself locked in the store cupboard.

"Let me out—it's not time for Postman's Knock yet, little ones!" he cried. Outside the door, the Inspector shrugged.

"Obviously a bluff," he said to himself. "Now for the other one!"

In a nearby room, the sports car

driver was putting on a black mask and cloak. He did not hear the Inspector as his soft shoes crept over the floorboards towards him.

"Ah ha! Your disguise does not fool me!" he chuckled, lungeing at the other man. He tripped over a chair and managed to bring down his adversary by one leg. There was a yell, and forty small children rushed into the room just as the Inspector's groping hands found the parcel he had driven so recklessly to find.

"Oh look—Pass The Parcel!" cried one small boy and, grabbing it from the Inspector's fingers, he made off with it.

"Hey, you!" gasped Clouseau, scrambling to his feet and chasing after the boy. Alarmed by this, the boy ran faster. All the other children, thinking it to be a new game, ran too.

The Inspector lost his footing at the top of the stairs and rolled all the way down to the street again. With him, however, went the parcel—and the boy ran back to join the party, wailing that someone had stolen one of the party prizes, and where was the vicar?

Chuckling with success, Clouseau jumped into his car and made off back up the road, failing to notice that he had swung the wrong way into a one way street.

"That's him, sir!" cried a nearby policeman into his walkie talkie. "Shall we go after him?"

The Inspector was very surprised, on his arrival back at the station, to find himself with an escort. Waving to them all, he ran quickly up the steps, leaving them all with open mouths as they realised who it was they'd been chasing. Inside, he found the sleepy station that he had left earlier that same afternoon transformed into a buzzing hive of activity, with the Chief in the centre of it all, tearing his hair as he stuck pins into maps, answered phones, and charted routes on maps.

"There's a maniac on the loose out there!" the Chief shouted at him as he walked in. "Good thing you came back, Inspector! We certainly need your help!"

The Inspector placed the parcel very carefully on his desk and told everyone to stand back. Then the Chief sent for the bomb squad and everyone took cover while the parcel was checked out for incendiary devices. It turned out to be quite an innocent package.

"You open it, sir," said the Inspector proudly, when, by nightfall, all the other people involved in the search were combing the area for the maniac. The Chief carefully undid the last wrapper.

"It may be diamonds," he said, opening the box inside. "Eh? What's this, Inspector—some sort of joke?"

The box was full of the remains of someone's picnic lunch. There were an awful lot of banana skins.

"Just where were you this afternoon, Inspector?" said the Chief in a dangerously quiet voice. "You wouldn't have had anything to do with that accident involving a busload of apes on an outing from the zoo, would you, by any chance?"

"Er . . . well, it was like this . . ." began Clouseau. He looked once more at the pile of banana skins in front of him. "I think you could say there's been some sort of a slip up, sir!"

Think Pink

Enter the spy-starred world of the Pink Panther yourself, with the secret spy's armoury of a good disguise while out on a mission! Bluff your enemies and keep the public guessing. It's a game that you can play anywhere, with as many friends as you can get to join in!

Newspapers: No good spy goes anywhere without a newspaper or a magazine. Not only does it give him something to read while waiting on street corners for a suspect to appear, but it is useful for hiding behind when watching someone discreetly in a cafe or some such place.

Large clothes: A coat that is too big for you can make you look totally different; you can tie a cushion around yourself under it to look like a fat person. Of course, this is not as effective if you are a large person already; so this should be used only by people who are thin.

Easy Ones

Collars: Always keep your collar turned up, to conceal your face. This can be difficult in summer when you haven't got a coat on, but is a simple winter disguise.

Hats: The bigger the better. A wide-brimmed hat in summer can be pulled down to make up for not having a collar to pull up. However, if you wear the same one too often you will be in danger of being recognised by the hat alone. This will never do, so build up a good collection of hats so that you can keep changing them. Jumble sales are good sources of new hats at very little cost.

Sunglasses: These hide the face and so are very good as a disguise; but if you wear them in dreary weather you will only draw attention to yourself, so their use is limited.

Clever Ones

Foreign costumes: Arab costumes are easy to make, using shepherd costumes from the school Nativity play and a teatowel around your head, kept in place with a piece of thick rope. The choice of teatowel could let you down here, so be careful; no self-respecting Arab would wear one with scenes from Majestic London on it, for example.

This sort of disguise should only be worn when you want to get past someone who might otherwise recognise you. Otherwise, it is best to choose a disguise which will help you merge into the background and look like everyone else around you.

Such as . . .

Fisherman: If you are playing this at the seaside, see what the locals are wearing. A bobble hat in a dull sort of colour, an old jersey, jeans and Wellington boots may be all you need to merge into the general scene.

Jogger: This is good for running away. Under whatever you are wearing, be dressed in a tee-shirt and shorts or start off wearing something light and add a track-suit on top. You should also have about your person a jogging wig (tell you about that in a minute) to put on before you jog past the suspect.

Good Props

These things will all help you to look like someone else.

False beard: Join together two pipe-cleaners and stitch some cotton wool in a beard shape to the middle of it. Carefully slosh some brown paint all over the beard to make it look more realistic and less like Father Christmas's, and leave it to dry. When it is, try it on by hooking the ends of the pipe-cleaners over your ears, making sure that it sits on your chin just under your bottom lip.

False moustache: A painted-on moustache is the safest. Anything else might fall off. But if you want a bushy type, use strands of wool stuck onto a piece of card, and attach it with a piece of sticky tape which you have folded back on itself so that it is sticky on both sides.

Jogging wig: You need lots of wool in a colour that is not your own hair colour. If you haven't got new wool, unpick an old black, brown or yellow jersey. Make yourself a headband to fit snugly round your head—this can be just a strip of material folded up and tied at the back. Taking long strands of wool, sew them to the inside of the head-band in a long fringe all round, and fill in the top loosely enough to fit on to your head (see diagram). As you jog past, this will look like real hair.

Other things which can be useful are: Large shopping bag; Camera (pretend to be a tourist and cover your face with the camera as if you are photographing something); Fishing rod and bag (for the person who wants to loiter by a stream to observe someone); Umbrella (for cover or self-protection).

A PANTHER SPECIAL
PLATFORM 2
THAT PANTHER'S DRIVING ME CRAZY! A HOLIDAY IS MY LAST CHANCE OF STAYING SANE.
PEACE, PANTHERLESS PEACE!
THE PANTHER WAS ALSO ENJOYING A TRAIN RIDE...
A NEW LIFE! JUST WHAT I NEED. NEW CHALLENGES, NEW HORIZONS.
STATION MA
ALL CHANGE! END OF LINE.
OH, NO!!
WHY, HALLO!

TAXI
PHEW! I'VE THROWN HIM OFF! HE'LL NEVER FIND ME HERE AT SUCH AN EXPENSIVE HOTEL
RITZ
RITZ
HOTEL RITZ
LITTLE DID HE KNOW THAT AT THE TRADESMEN'S ENTRANCE
THIS LOOKS LIKE THE JOINT!
I'M LOOKING FORWARD TO MY NEW JOB!
MAGNIFIQUE, EXCELLENT! A LITTLE OF THIS! A LOT OF THAT!
MENU
HA, HA! I AM THE NEW WAITER, AND YOU, SIR, SHALL HAVE SPECIAL TREATMENT.
GROAN!
YOUR SOUP, SIR!

AARGH!!
I THINK YOU'RE SUPPOSED TO USE THE SPOON IN A POSH PLACE LIKE THIS IF YOU DON'T MIND ME SAYING SO, SIR!
URK!
IT MUST ALL BE A TERRIBLE DREAM; NO-ONE COULD BE SO UNLUCKY AS TO SPEND HIS HOLIDAY NEAR THE PINK PANTHER
AARGH! WHAT I NEED IS A NIGHTMARE TO GET ME OVER THE SHOCK OF THE REALITY.
THE INSPECTOR HEADS FOR THE SEA
TO BEACH
WHAT DO I CARE ABOUT THE PANTHER? HE'S WORKING, I'M NOT! I SHALL BASK IN THE SUN.
DECK CHAIRS
LIKE TO HIRE A DECK-CHAIR, SIR?

YOU'RE SUPPOSED TO BE WORKING IN THE HOTEL!
OH, THIS IS JUST A LITTLE FILL-IN JOB UNTIL LUNCH
HERE'S A SPECIAL ONE JUST FOR YOU.- IT'S GOT ARMS.
I DON'T WANT IT!
HELP!
UMPH!
ARGH!
I THINK YOU'D BETTER COME WITH US, SIR.
IT WAS THIS MAN! HE ASSAULTED THE DECK-CHAIR ATTENDANT.
YOU'VE GOT IT WRONG! I'M ONE OF YOU!
SOME PEOPLE JUST DON'T KNOW HOW TO ENJOY THEMSELVES, DO THEY?

Pink Professions

The charm and sophistication of the Pink Panther may well have prompted you to think of working with animals as a career. If so, pinkly peruse the following . . .

Zoo Keeper

Lots of people are needed in zoos to keep the animals fit and healthy and clean. If you have ever thought about working in a zoo at all, your view of it may have been limited to visions of yourself throwing large lumps of meat through the bars to huge animals and then watching to make sure that they can't get out of their cages. In real life there is a lot more to the job than this and to start with a keeper needs to be quite knowledgeable about animals, especially the sort he is looking after. Also it helps to have a background knowledge of nutrition so that you know why animals must eat certain foods and avoid others. You need to be very patient and extremely reliable, prepared to work in all weathers in sometimes difficult conditions.

Still keen? Then write to the Head Keeper of the group of animals you would like to work with most, or if you are not sure which would interest you more than any other, send your letter to the curator of whichever zoo you choose. If you write well before you leave school—even before you get to your last year—telling them that you would like to work in the zoo as a keeper, and asking how to go about it, you will have plenty of time to plan your next move when they have told you what to do. Send a stamped addressed envelope for their reply.

Aim high; try for the better zoos and ignore the sort of zoo that is just a tourist attraction at the seaside, with animals kept in poor conditions and open to the public in the summer only. If you really love animals you will become very depressed indeed working in such a place, which will be worse than not working at all.

Shepherd

Did you know that many girls are becoming shepherds now? This is because the job has become more mechanised and so a man's strength is not as important as once it was in this life. All the same, you do need to be pretty fit and fond of the outdoor life.

Lambing is the most dangerous and exhausting time of the shepherd's year, and of course it is the most important time too, as a good crop of lambs is essential for financial success on the farm. Shearing-time means a lot of hard work too, as the sheep have to be turned over during shearing. Large farms may employ professional shearers but in small places the shepherd and the farmer will do the job between them.

The most rewaıding part of being a shepherd may well be the relationship you have with a good sheepdog; working together well can give you a great sense of fulfilment in your work. You can start on a farm as a general labourer, specialising when the opportunity arises—or you can apply for a place in an agricultural college and learn enough to enable you to leave with a diploma, which could help you to get a job with sheep more easily.

Animal Shelters

Both the PDSA and the RSPCA run cat and dog shelters where strays are looked after and if you are good with animals this could be the job for you. Finding out if there is such a shelter near you should not be too difficult, but only think of applying for a job if you are reliable enough to arrive on time and work hard. The same thing applies to the sort of kennels where owners pay to leave their pets while they go on holiday. If animals are relying on you to look after them you must not let them down.

The work will be quite simple—cleaning out the sleeping quarters, feeding the animals and helping to nurse them if they are sick. For this reason it may turn out to be a very limiting sort of job, but working with live creatures has its own rewards.

Riding Stables

Your chance of getting a job in a riding stables will depend on a lot of things—if it can afford to employ help at all. As a career its possibilities are limited and you could soon be looking for a place with more responsibility, but it is certainly no bad thing to get to know the people at your riding stable while you are still at school and offer your help at weekends and during the holidays. You might get paid for this in free lessons rather than hard cash; anyway, it is good experience if you want to get to know horses and how to look after them and their equipment.

Here are some other jobs with animals:

Police dog handler
Racing stable lad
Pet shop assistant
RSPCA Inspector
Veterinary surgeon or nurse

PINK PATHWAYS

Join the Smug Panther in the centre of this maze – if you can. He's pleased with himself for finding the way in – can you do it too?

The Pink Panther had decided that a complete and total break was just what he needed.

"Far away from all the pressures and strains of everyday life," he mused. "I haven't had a holiday for so long that I can't remember where I've been."

Strolling down to the travel agent took but a few minutes. The travel agent thrust some brochures at him.

"What about these, sir? Mountaineering in the Bavarian Alps. Just the thing, I would have thought."

"Oh, that's just the thing," agreed the Panther. Being a creature of impulse, he paid up on the spot and went home to pack his bags.

It was hot on the plane, and the flight seemed to take forever. At last they landed and a rickety bus took them halfway up a mountain until they arrived at a very grand and impressive castle, out on the hillside.

"Isn't that the most perfect place to spend a holiday?" breathed a fat lady in the seat next to the Panther.

"It certainly looks like it, madam," replied the Panther. "But I'll see what it's like on the inside before I decide. I don't really care what it's like from here; it's what the food and beds are like that interests me."

"Oh, how droll you are!" cried the lady, going into peals of laughter. "But you're quite right, of course. However, I have a certain talent for the ancient art of sorcery, and I feel sure that it will all be wonderful in there."

"You mean you're an old witch?" asked the Panther politely.

The lady's expression changed. "No I do not!" she shrieked, and hit him over the head with her handbag, which opened and tipped its contents all over the Panther and the floor of the bus.

At the same moment the bus jolted to a stop outside the front door of the castle and there was a mad stampede to be first off the stuffy vehicle.

The Panther's room was quite ordinary but it did have an ancient bathroom, equipped with an ancient bath, adjoining it. Tired and sticky, the Panther decided that a bath was essential after the journey, especially as some of the perfume and other unidentifiable material from the fat lady's handbag had lodged about his ears and throat. When he went to run the bath, however, he found a large green frog sitting in it.

"Bother!" said the Panther. "One might expect to have one's bath to oneself without having to share with toads and other impedimentia."

"Excuse me, but I am not a toad," replied the frog. The Panther stared, amazed.

"A talking frog!" he cried.

"Why not?" said the frog. "After all, you're a talking panther . . . and what's worse, you're pink. At least I'm a normal sort of colour."

"Who says pink is any less normal a colour than green?" protested the Panther.

"I daresay you have a point—in general," said the frog. "All I'm saying is that while pink is a very strange colour for panthers, green is quite normal for frogs."

"You have me there," admitted the Panther. "But tell me—why have I got you here? In my bath?"

"Didn't you read the brochures?" asked the frog. "Didn't you know that you were coming to a fairytale hotel?"

"Oh yes, I read all that," said the Panther impatiently. "But never for one brief moment did I associate the term with the likelihood of finding a frog occupying my quarters—or even my eighths or sixteenths. Why should I?"

"Dear me, you're no detective, are you, sir?" the frog went on. "Fairytales—frogs. You always get frogs in fairytales, if they're any good, that is."

The Panther, failing to understand this, and feeling that if he asked any more questions he would never get his bath, disappeared into the bathroom and ran some hot water. For a while he wallowed in the delicious luxury of a much-needed soak, and when he emerged some time later it was to find that the frog had totally vanished, and along with him all the Panther's own monogrammed silk pyjamas and other clothes. In their place were several garments of a very . . . *unusual* style, none of which would have been the Panther's own choice on any shopping trip that he might have made in his right mind.

Finding nothing else to put on he decided that it must be a fancydress evening in the ballroom and put on the knickerbockers, jerkin and cloak which were laid out, along with the fancy buckled slippers on the mat. Feeling rather peckish by this time, he stepped out down the corridor in search of the dining-room.

"Oh for a piping hot pie or two, some bread and cheese and some wine would do," he sang to himself as he looked for the lift. "Ah, here we are—the lift doors approach!"

He pressed the down button and a lift appeared. The doors opened and he got in. There was no one else in the lift. The Panther pressed the button for the ground floor and the doors glided shut once more. There was a sudden rush in the Panther's ears and the lift whizzed off again.

"Funny," thought the Panther. "I could have sworn we were going up instead of down."

The lights in the lift flickered and in the temporary darkness he noticed that his own paw was glittering with a strange brightness all of its own. "It's that stuff from that woman's handbag," he muttered to himself. "Let's hope I don't reek of some awful smell when I'm mingling with all the other guests."

Thinking thoughts like these he automatically got out when the lift stopped, without thinking to check that it was the right floor. By the time he had found out that it wasn't, it was much too late and the lift had disappeared.

"Better look for the stairs," thought the Panther, and wandered off along the corridor. There was a large door ahead so he went through it.

He was standing in a massive ballroom which appeared to have been the scene of a wild rave-up.

"The local wine must be really strong here," thought the Panther. "It's sent everyone to sleep! You'd think they could get someone in to do some cleaning-up before they start having parties though," he mused, looking with distaste at the cobwebs and dust everywhere. "Whoops! Sorry, madam, I didn't see you there."

He backed off from the snoozing lady he had just bumped into, and fell backwards over a sleeping dog. Losing his footing completely he fell flat on his face, this time right on top of a beautiful girl.

"Tch!" said the Panther, sitting up. "Dreadfully sorry, and all that. Wasn't meaning to take liberties."

The girl opened her eyes and smiled up at him. "Where's my prince? He kissed me!" she said dreamily.

"Not I," said the Panther. "I sneezed while tripping over you, that's all. It's the dust, you know."

"It certainly was not," said the frog, popping up beside him quite suddenly, and glaring at him with the nastiest green glare the Panther had ever seen.

"Thank goodness for that," said the beautiful girl, sitting up and stretching. "I thought I was going to have to go back to sleep again. It happened once before, you know.

How wonderful! My prince at last!"

Flinging her arms round his neck, she embraced the Pink Panther and kissed him noisily on the cheek.

"Jolly good show," said a fat man in a crown. "Nice to have you for a son-in-law. Let's organise some food and we'll have a chat about which state department you'd like to run. Lark curry all right? The cook should be able to rustle some up out of the leftovers."

"Oh Daddy, you are behind the times," laughed the beautiful girl. "Nobody eats larks any more! It'll have to be chicken, I'm afraid."

"My little girl will make a wonderful wife," smirked someone who was obviously the Queen. "Regal as anything, but beautiful with it and so handy in the kitchen! You won't regret it at all, I'm sure."

The Panther blinked. "Me? Getting married?"

"Let's have a party!" said the king, and all the courtiers yelled loudly in approval, sending the royal party helter-skelter down the staircase.

Down in the foyer was a big notice, which the Panther had not bothered to read on his way in. Now he could see that it said: VISIT THE SLEEPING BEAUTY'S CASTLE AND TRY YOUR LUCK AT WAKING HER UP—ONLY £1 A KISS!

Light dawned in the Panther's mind. Turning to the frog he remarked: "Is this the Princess who's the Sleeping Beauty?"

"That's her," said the frog. "Only

she's not the Sleeping Beauty now you've woken her up."

"Oh no!" said the Panther. He was beginning to realise what it all meant now. His entire future was mapped out for him. Was royalty his scene? He wasn't too sure. And it seemed that he didn't have much choice.

The lad who had given him his room key ran over to him and looked at the number on it as it dangled from the Panther's paw.

"The lucky number is Room 227!" he cried. "We have a winner!"

Suddenly a very angry weasel of a man ran out from a back room. "It's all a mistake!" he cried. "This person hasn't bought a ticket! He's kissed the Princess without paying! It's all a swindle, and nobody should have woken up at all! Get back to sleep, everyone. Go on! I'm the manager here, and you'd better do as I say!"

"Look here, mister," snarled the fat king, his face going an odd shade of red as he got angrier. "This is my castle and I'm King in it, so now I'm awake *I* hand out the orders. I don't know where you've come from but I know where you're going . . ."

"Calm down, everyone," said the Panther, springing between them just in time. "There are ladies present, you know."

"My hero!" cried the Princess delightedly.

"This is my castle now," said the manager snootily. "I rent it from the Tourist Board and all the electricity bills are up to date, so I'm not budging for anyone."

"What do you mean, you rent it from the Tourist Board?" thundered the King. "No board has the right! I'll floor any board that tries it!"

The manager began to snivel.

"What am I going to tell the guests?" he wailed. "No Sleeping Beauty! No Court At Rest! No Wake-The-Princess Competition!"

"Look out, boss," said the page-boy quietly. "Here they all come now—down the spiral staircase."

Everyone looked upwards. The Panther could see, in the middle of his fellow-travellers, the fat lady who had spilled her handbag over him. There was a strange gleam in her amber eyes which he had not noticed before.

"That's it!" he muttered. "It must have been that perfume which spilled over me that gave me the power to wake the Princess!"

"Of course it was," said the frog impatiently. "How could anyone help but wake up with that awful pong up her nose? And it was guaranteed to give you the special princely powers, too. Just don't have a bath from now on, that's all. One wash—and that's it."

"But I've *had* a bath!" cried the Panther. "Don't you remember? I had to move you out of it first!"

The frog hopped backwards and looked at the Panther with new respect.

"I'd forgotten that," he said. "So most of it had been washed off! You must have been the real prince all along!"

By now the guests had arrived at the bottom of the staircase and were marching angrily over to the hotel manager.

"Look here, we're hungry!" one of them shouted.

"Yes, and we can't find the dining-room!" cried another.

"The service here is appalling!" yelled a third.

"Quiet, everyone!" bellowed the King. There was immediate silence.

"I regret the mix-up," said the King, more quietly. "My manager has had rather a difficult day. However, a feast is being prepared at this very moment to celebrate the engagement of my lovely daughter the Princess to her newly-found Prince, so if you will follow me, I will instruct the Court musicians to play some soothing music for however long it takes for . . . er . . . chicken curry to be prepared. Come, everyone!"

"Trust your father to recognise a way of making money when he sees one," said the Queen to the Princess. She leaned forward to the Panther. "Look lively—you'd better help us

get it all ready in the kitchen!"

"What about the cook?" asked the Panther weakly.

"I *am* the cook!" roared the Queen. "And you're my new kitchen-maid!"

"Oh help!" sighed the Panther. "This is turning into Cinderella, not the Sleeping Beauty!"

"Don't worry," said the frog. "It's only until the morning, when the new staff comes on duty."

"You mean it isn't all a dream?" asked the Panther.

"Certainly not," said the frog, as they made their way to the kitchens. "Don't you like it? I can tell you, I wish I'd been picked to be the prince. Just a dab of that perfume would have turned me into one, you know."

"I think that can be arranged," said the Panther. "Nip upstairs with me now and I think you'll find that some of it landed in my toothbrush container. It might just be enough to do the trick."

"What are we waiting for?" asked the frog. Together they slipped unnoticed upstairs and found the toothbrush container.

"We're in luck," said the Panther. "Here goes! I'm pouring it . . . now!"

There was a sizzle, and the frog disappeared. In its place stood a green panther!

"Not quite what I expected," he said. "But it'll do, I suppose. The lights aren't all that good downstairs, so I don't think the Princess will notice the difference. What will you do now?"

"Get out as fast as possible!" said the Pink Panther. "Goodbye!"

Knotting together several sheets, he made a quick descent to the ground outside and ran like mad for the far horizon.

Holidays? The Pink Panther had done with holidays!

Pink Playtime

Secret Parcel

Wrap up a match box as a secret parcel. The idea of the game is to secretly pass this box to another player while you are out in public—in the street, in the park, without anyone else knowing. Start by drawing lots for who is first to carry the parcel. You can do this by taking a drinking straw for everyone who is playing and putting them all together in a beaker. One of the straws must have a small rolled-up piece of paper in the end that can't be seen. Everyone shuts his eyes and draws a straw, placing it in his pocket while keeping his eyes closed. When everyone is ready, eyes can be opened, and each person secretly looks at his straw to see if it is the one with the paper in it. He tells no one, but when everyone has wandered off he goes to the place where the box has been hidden and takes it away, looking for someone else to pass it to. Meanwhile, everyone with ordinary straws has to try not to be spotted, so that the box-carrier cannot pass it to them. This is where the good disguise comes in!

Make a note of who you passed the box to and at what time of day (if you can). Have a fixed time to stop—say four o'clock in the afternoon, for example, and all meet to see where the box has been all day. You can add your own rules to this—for instance, no one should be allowed to travel outside a certain area but must remain in the vicinity so as not to unfairly avoid being spotted. Also, at any point you can end the game by catching two players red-handed in the act of passing the box over.

Anyone doing this must be sure that the others are within calling distance, however—so that he can call the game to an end. Otherwise there is nothing to stop the two caught redhanded from running away and leaving him with the box to pass on again!

Whispering

Find a fellow player and whisper a message in his ear. You must say it only once and may not repeat any part of it. At the same time, give him a list of names of everyone playing. Your name is on it first, and his second; he must then run to the third person on the list and whisper the message (as he has heard it) in that person's ear. He then takes the list and whispers the message in the ear of the next person listed, and so on until all players have been whispered to. Then everyone gets together and the last players tells the first player what he thought the message was. It will probably be vastly different from the original message, and great fun can be had by tracing where it went wrong!

Answers to pages 34 and 35

1

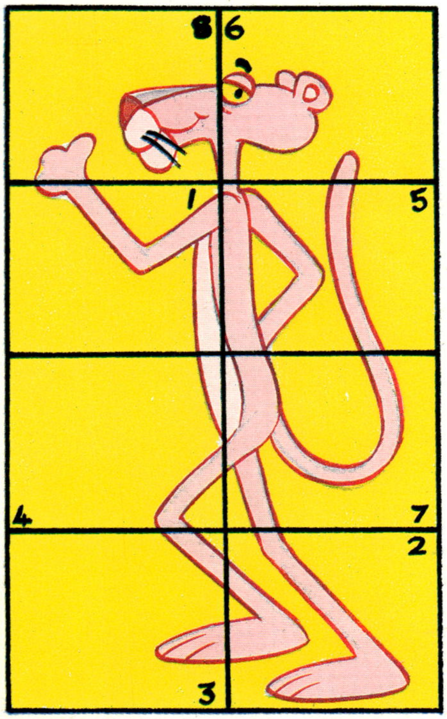

2 The black circles show the coins to be moved. The broken-line circles show where they must be replaced.

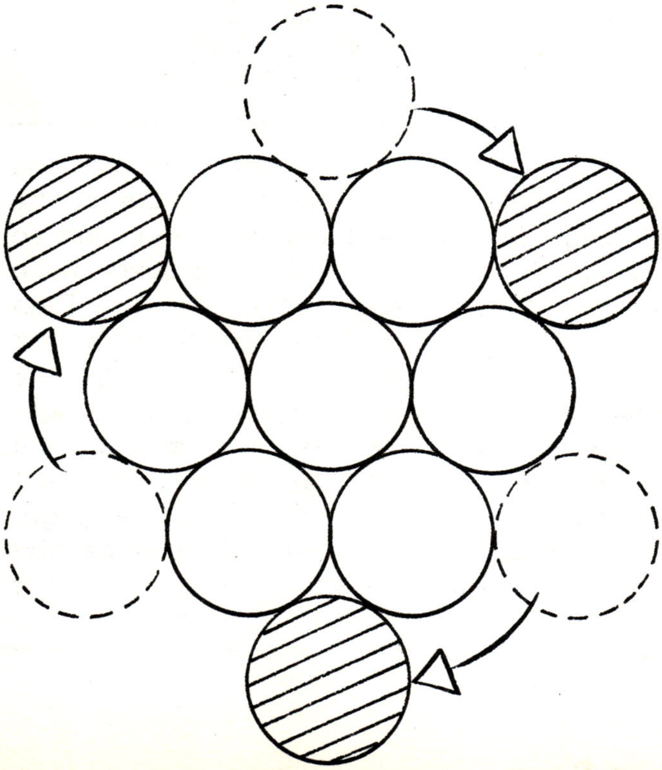

3 Before you start to draw, make a tiny crease in the paper. Above this, draw an eye, carrying on to the second half of the paper for the mouth and drawing a matching eye above the other end of the smile. Keeping the pencil on the paper, open out the paper and draw in the hair and chin. It doesn't matter that you go over part of your drawing to make the picture complete.

4 BANJO
GUITAR
MANDOLIN
FLUTE
PIANO
OBOE
HARPSICHORD
VIOLIN

5 No. 3 is different.

6 It's a snowman!

PINK PANTHER RULES